Budget Recipes for One

Single Serving Desserts

From the Series:

Budget Recipes for One – The Art of Cooking for Yourself

DISCLAIMER

All information in the book is for general information purposes only.

The author has used her best efforts in preparing this information and makes no representations or warranties with respect to the accuracy, applicability or completeness of the material contained within.

Furthermore, the author takes no responsibility for any errors, omissions or inaccuracies in this document. The author disclaims any implied or expressed warranties or fitness for any particular purpose.

The author shall in no event be held liable for losses or damages whatsoever. The author assumes no responsibility or liability for any consequences resulting directly or indirectly from any action or lack of action that you take based on the information in this document.

Use of the publication and recipes therein is at your own risk.

Reproduction or translation of any part of this publication by any means, electronic or mechanical, without the permission of the author, is both forbidden and illegal. You are not permitted to share, sell, and trade or give away this document and it is for your own personal use only, unless stated otherwise.

By using any of the recipes in this publication, you agree that you have read the disclaimer and agree with all the terms.

The reader assumes full risk and responsibility for all actions taken as a result of the information contained within this book and the author will not be held responsible for any loss or damage, whether consequential, incidental, or otherwise that may result from the information presented in this book.

The author has relied on her own experiences when compiling this book and each recipe is tried and tested in her own kitchen.

Table of Contents

Introduction

Homemade desserts are something that I nearly gave up on altogether after my children left home. It seemed silly to spend time making the desserts that I had previously made for four or five people only to end up having to eat the same dessert myself for a few days. There are some delicious looking desserts and puddings in the supermarkets but I like to know what ingredients are in the food I am eating so prefer to make my own with fresh ingredients when possible.

I absolutely love sweet stuff so I decided to research and adapt some desserts that I could make just for myself but at the same time, were easy to increase for when I had visitors.

The following pages are the results of my labors. There are different types of desserts from baked to frozen, cakes and sweets to hot puddings – and I love them all...

My aim with this series of **Cooking for One** books is to document quick and easy recipes that even a novice cook will easily be able to replicate. Sure, there are thousands of cookbooks on the market but, in my experience, most are trying to invent new recipes. I have tried to include well-known food that a beginner may be familiar with but not know how to make. Almost all the recipes in this book are simple to make.

I am also trying to encourage people to experiment with tastes and ingredients to find food they will enjoy and, more importantly, make again. After all, it's no good buying a cookbook and leaving it on the shelf (or unused on your Kindle), I want to encourage people to cook meals, both savory and sweet, from scratch rather than buying processed food that is full of additives and preservatives from the supermarket.

I have tried, where possible, to use American weights and measures (please forgive me if I get some wrong – I'm British...) but have included a simple conversion chart at the end of the book for European readers.

Another point to be aware of if you are not in America is that a couple of the branded ingredients listed may be difficult to source in your country, so improvise and experiment – I did. At the end of the book I have included a short list of some possible substitutes for the American products along with European names for some American terms – I hope this helps.

I hope this '**Budget Cooking for One – Single Serving Desserts**' cook book helps you to create interesting, cheap and mouthwatering desserts that you will enjoy preparing and eating.

Blueberry Muffins

These muffins are simple to make and freeze really well. They are just as nice hot with cream or custard or cold with a cup of coffee.

The recipe makes 12 decent sized muffins so you can freeze 10 for a quick and easy snack when you feel like something sweet.

Defrost by popping in the microwave for 30 seconds or so – depending on your microwave.

Ingredients

14 oz all-purpose flour
7 oz of sugar
7fl oz buttermilk
3fl oz milk
2 eggs
1 teaspoon of good vanilla extract
3oz melted butter
Handful of your chosen fruit or chocolate chips

Method

Preheat oven to 220C.

Mix buttermilk, milk, vanilla extract and eggs together

Put sugar and flour in a large bowl, make a well in the center and stir in the liquid mix. Mix well but don't overdo it.

Add choc chips or fruit - as much or as little as you like, blueberries are brilliant as are diced apple, strawberries or raspberries. You can even use frozen fruit if you wish.

Use 12 large muffin cases. Use all the mix. Instead of adding your fruit to the mix you can fill the muffin cases and press the pieces of fruit into the mixture before baking.

Bake in the middle of the oven for around 20 minutes.

Ready when they are nicely colored and spongy to the touch.

Leave to cool on a rack and freeze what you don't want to eat right away.

These muffins are really moist and delicious either on their own as a snack or with custard as a pudding.

Single Serving Strawberry Cake

Ingredients

1 tablespoon sugar
3 tablespoon all-purpose flour
Pinch of salt
1 tablespoon plus 1 teaspoon milk
¼ teaspoon baking powder
1 or 2 tablespoon strawberries, chopped
1 tablespoon coconut oil
½ teaspoon vanilla extract

Method

Preheat oven to 330°F. Grease a ramekin well.

In a small bowl, mix together the flour, baking powder, sugar, vanilla extract and salt. Whisk in the milk and coconut oil.

Then toss in the strawberries and give a stir until just combined.

Pour the mixture into the prepared ramekin and bake for 15- 20 minutes until golden on the top.

Serve with ice cream or whipped cream.

Baked Sweet and Spicy Pear

Ingredients

1 pear, peeled, thinly sliced
2 tablespoon brown sugar
2 tablespoon quick-cooking oats
1 tablespoon flour
1/8 teaspoon cinnamon
1 tablespoon butter

Method

Place the sliced peach in the bottom of a ramekin.

In a small bowl, mix together the brown sugar, oats, cinnamon, butter and flour and add to the peach slices.

Using a spoon slightly flatten the top and bake in the oven for 25 minutes.

Delicious served with a generous drizzle of maple syrup.

Crème Brulee for One

Ingredients

½ cup heavy cream
1/8 cup sugar, plus
½ tablespoon sugar to caramelize
1 egg yolk
½ teaspoon vanilla extract

Method

Preheat oven to 300 °F (150°C).

Combine the heavy cream and sugar in a small saucepan and set over high heat. When it just begins to boil, remove from the heat.

In a small bowl, beat the egg yolk and vanilla. Then gradually whisk in the cream mixture, little at a time. Make sure not to add all the hot cream mixture at once as it will cook the egg yolk. Pour the mixture into a ramekin.

Transfer the ramekin to a deep rimmed baking tray. Pour enough water into a baking dish so it covers halfway the sides of the ramekin.

Bake in the oven for 40 minutes.

Then carefully remove the ramekin from the oven and let cool at room temperature.

Let chill for at least 2 hours. Just before you serve, sprinkle about tablespoon of sugar over the chilled ramekin and using a blow torch caramelize it. Alternatively, place the ramekin under hot grill for 2-3 minutes until the sugar is caramelized.

Banana and Pecan Sauce Cakes

Ingredients

For the sauce
1/8 cup light brown sugar
1½ tablespoons unsalted butter
1 small banana, sliced into circles
½ tablespoon pecans, toasted, chopped
For the cake
1 tablespoon unsalted butter, melted
1½ tablespoon granulated sugar
1 tablespoon Greek yogurt (or buttermilk)
¼ teaspoon ground cinnamon
1 egg yolk
¼ teaspoon vanilla extract
¼ teaspoon baking powder
1/5 cup flour

Method

Preheat the oven to 350°F.

Coat 4-5 cups in a muffin tray with cooking spray.

To make the sauce, in a small microwave safe bowl combine the brown sugar and butter and microwave until the butter is melted.

Add about 1 teaspoon of the sauce mixture into each of the prepared cups. Top with a circle or two of banana. Reserve any extra sauce for later use. Next, sprinkle a little chopped pecans over.

To make the batter for the cake, combine the yogurt, sugar, and melted butter in a bowl. Beat in the egg yolk and vanilla extract. In a separate bowl, mix together the flour, cinnamon and baking powder and add to the yogurt mixture and mix well.

Next, divide the batter between the muffin cups and bake in the oven for 10 minutes. Then remove the tin from the oven and let cool. Gently remove the cupcakes from the tin and enjoy with extra sauce and a few chopped pecan nuts drizzled over.

Chocolate Chip Berry Palova

Ingredients

1/8 cup powdered sugar
1 small egg white
Dash of cream of tartar
Dash of salt
½ tablespoon semisweet chocolate chips
1/8 teaspoon vanilla extract
¼ teaspoon granulated sugar
¼ cup your favorite berries, sliced
Whipped cream

Method

Preheat oven to 250° F.

Using a pencil, draw a 3-inch circle on the parchment paper and lay over baking sheet, drawn side down.

Put the egg white, cream of tartar, and salt into a small bowl and beat with an electric mixer at high speed. Then add the powdered sugar, about a tablespoon at a time, beating well after each addition until glossy stiff peaks form. Toss in the vanilla and chocolate chips.

Place the beaten egg white on the drawn circle and give a shape with a spoon.

Bake in the oven for 60-80 minutes until firm to the touch.

Turn off the oven and let the meringue stay in the oven for at least 2-3 hours.

In a bowl, mix together the berries and sugar. Carefully remove the meringue from the paper and place in a serving plate. Spread with whipped cream then top with the berry mixture and enjoy.

The beauty of this recipe is you can use any berry you like or even combine a few different ones for an added bit of luxury. For an extra quick dessert you could use the shop-bought meringue nests and add your own topping.

Apple Cobbler for One

Ingredients

1/3 cup sugar
1 tablespoon butter, melted
1/3 cup flour
½ teaspoon baking powder
1/3 cup milk
Pinch salt
1 apple, peeled, thinly sliced
½ teaspoon vanilla sugar

Method

Place the butter in a small casserole dish and melt over low heat.

In a small bowl, combine the flour, sugar, milk, salt and baking powder and pour the batter into the casserole.

Sprinkle the sliced apple with vanilla sugar and toss to coat. Then place the apples on the top of the batter and transfer to the oven.

Bake until the top becomes golden brown, about 40-45 minutes.

Let cool and enjoy with a big dollop of whipped cream.

Chocolate Chip Cookie for One

Ingredients

1 tablespoon white sugar
1 tablespoon brown sugar
1 tablespoon butter
1 tablespoon water
1/8 teaspoon vanilla
1 pinch salt
1 pinch baking soda
¼ cup flour
Extra flour for dusting hands and board
1-2 tablespoon chocolate chips

Method

Preheat oven to 350 °F.

In a small bowl, mix together the butter, white and brown sugars, water and flour. Add the baking soda, salt, vanilla and chocolate chips and mix well to combine.

Gently coat the baking sheet with cooking spray and place the dough onto it.

Dust your hands with flour, flatten the dough and shape a round

Bake in the oven for about 13 minutes.

Remove from the oven and let cool.

Note: These keep well in an airtight container so it is worth doubling up the recipe and making more for later.

Cinnamon Streusel Cake for One

Ingredients

For the cake:
2 tablespoon sugar
2 tablespoon plain yogurt
1 egg white
2½ tablespoon flour
1/8 teaspoon baking powder
1/8 teaspoon salt
¼ teaspoon vanilla

For the streusel: (streusel is a crumbly topping of
flour, butter, and sugar that is baked on top of muffins,
breads, pies, and cakes)
2 tablespoon butter, cut into small cubes
2 tablespoon brown sugar
1 tablespoon flour
½ teaspoon cinnamon

Method

Preheat oven to 350°F. Take a wide-mouth
mason jar or a ramekin and spray with cooking
spray.

In a small bowl, beat the egg white, sugar,
vanilla and yogurt. Add the flour, salt and baking
powder and mix until smooth.

To make the streusel, take a small bowl and combine the cubed butter, cinnamon, sugar and flour. Mix with your hands until the mixture resembles fine crumbs.

Add ½ of the batter to the jar, and then add about 1/3 of the streusel mixture.

Then add the remaining batter followed by the remaining streusel mixture.

Bake in the oven for about 20-22 minutes, until the top is golden and a toothpick inserted in the center comes out clean.

Let cool and enjoy with custard or cream.

Desert Island Parfait

Ingredients

¼ cup mango, chopped
½ banana, sliced into circles
¼ cup pineapple, chopped
3 drops coconut extracts
1 (6 oz.) container vanilla yogurt
2 tablespoon whipped cream
1 teaspoon sweetened coconut, shredded

Method

Drop the coconut extract into the yogurt and stir well to combine.

Pour half of the yogurt into a serving glass, place half of the chopped mango, half of the chopped pineapple on the top, followed by half of the banana circles.

Then add the remaining yogurt and top again with chopped fruit layers.

Top with the whipped cream. Place in refrigerator for an hour or so to chill then sprinkle with shredded coconut and enjoy.

Note: you can use any fruit you like for this and, for a truly decadent dessert, substitute the yoghurt for whipped cream and top with grated chocolate.

Blueberry Crumble

Ingredients

½ cup frozen blueberries
½ teaspoon lemon juice
1 teaspoon sugar
½ teaspoon arrowroot starch
2 tablespoon oats
2 tablespoon chopped walnuts
1 teaspoon almond flour
1/8 teaspoon cinnamon
½ tablespoon butter, melted

Method

Preheat oven to 350°F.

Place the blueberries, sugar, arrowroot starch in a small bowl, drizzle with lemon juice and gently toss until blueberries are well coated. Place the mixture into a small ovenproof dish.

In a small bowl, combine the walnuts, oats, cinnamon and almond flour. Add the butter and rub well in with your fingers. Once the mixture gets crumbly spread evenly over the blueberry mixture.

Transfer to the oven and bake for 10-12 minutes until the top is golden.

Let cool and enjoy with cream or custard.

Lemon and Carrot Cake for One

Ingredients

4 oz extra fine sugar
4 oz all-purpose flour
4 oz butter
2 free-range eggs
1 carrot, grated
1 tablespoon milk
1 lemon, zest and juice
Butter, for greasing

Method

Put the sugar and butter to a bowl and beat until light and creamy.

Whisk in the eggs, milk and flour followed by the carrot, lemon zest and juice. Beat until well blended.

Grease one or two ramekins and pour the prepared batter into it.

Transfer to the microwave and bake for about 3 minutes on High.

Microwave Berry Cobbler

Ingredients

¾ cup strawberries, chopped (or any berry you
    prefer)
¼ cup powdered sugar
1/3 cup flour
1 tablespoon white sugar
½ teaspoon baking powder
1 tablespoon butter
2 tablespoon milk

Method

Place the chopped strawberries in a mug. Stir
in the powdered sugar.

Mix the white sugar, flour, baking powder
together in a small bowl.

Next, add the butter and mix in well with your
fingers. Then stir in the milk.

Place the dough over the berries and microwave
for 2 minutes on High.

Let cool and enjoy.

Quick Cinnamon Apple Treat

Ingredients

1 large Granny Smith apple, peeled, cored and chopped
3 teaspoon sugar
½ teaspoon cinnamon
1 teaspoon cornstarch
¼ cup water
1 tablespoon whipped cream
Cinnamon graham cracker, crumbled

Method

Place the chopped apple, cinnamon, cornstarch and sugar in a medium pan and set over medium heat. Let cook for 5 minutes, stirring frequently.

Once the sugar is caramelized, add the water and continue cooking for another 8-9 minutes, stirring occasionally until the water has reduced.

Spoon the mixture into a serving glass and top with whipped cream.

Sprinkle the graham cracker crumbs over and enjoy.

Ginger Cranberry Pear

Ingredients

1 small pear, peeled, cut into ¾ inch pieces
1/8 cup dried cranberries
1½ tablespoon sugar
1 teaspoon all-purpose flour
½ teaspoon fresh ginger, grated
Pinch ground cinnamon
1 tablespoon butter
Topping
1½ tablespoon sugar
½ teaspoon fresh ginger, grated
¼ cup all-purpose flour
1/8 teaspoon baking soda
Pinch of salt
1 tablespoon cold butter
1/8 cup buttermilk

Method

Preheat oven to 350°F

Place the cranberries, pear, sugar, grated ginger, cinnamon and flour in a bowl and mix well to combine.

Grease a custard cup or a ramekin and place the pear mixture into it. Cut the butter into small pieces and sprinkle over the pear.

Place in the oven and bake for 15-20 minutes until bubbling.

To make the topping, blend the sugar and ginger in a blender until crumbs form. Take and reserve about 1 teaspoon of the mixture. And then add salt, flour, and baking soda to the blender. Pulse for 15-20 seconds. Lastly throw in the butter and blend until crumbly.

Place the flour mixture in a bowl. Add the buttermilk and mix well. Spoon the mixture over the baked fruit filling and top with the reserved sugar mixture.

Bake in the oven for about 35 minutes until the topping acquires golden crust.

Enjoy warm.

Almond Raspberry Muffin for One

Ingredients

5 tablespoon all-purpose flour
¼ teaspoon baking powder
1 tablespoon ground almonds
2 tablespoons brown sugar
Pinch of salt
3 tablespoon milk
2 tablespoons vegetable oil
2 tablespoons dark chocolate chips
5-6 raspberries

Method

Preheat oven to 440 °F (225°C). Grease a ramekin.

Place the flour, baking powder, almonds, brown sugar, salt and chocolate chips in a small bowl and mix.

Whisk in the oil and milk. Once the batter is well combined, pour half of it into the ramekin. Place the raspberries on the top and push with your fingers.

Add the remaining batter.

Place in the preheated oven and bake for 5 minutes, then reduce the heat to 400 °F (200°C) and continue baking for another 15-20 minutes. If the top is getting dark brown, cover with foil to prevent from burning. Cooked when a skewer comes out clean when inserted into center.

Leave to cool then ease from ramekin and enjoy.

Baked Apple with Blackberries

I usually make these when blackberries are in season and I've been out picking them from the bushes near my home – free is my favorite price!

Ingredients

1 medium apple
1 tablespoon walnuts, finely chopped
1 tablespoon agave or maple syrup
1 teaspoon ground cinnamon
Handful blackberries with a few extra for garnish

Method

Preheat the oven to 350°F (180°C).

Using a small sharp knife, core the apple, removing seeds. This is to open a hole for the filling. To avoid the apple bursting score a line all the way round the middle of the apple with the knife. To make a bigger cavity you could slice the top off the apple and remove the core and a bit more of the apple flesh, chop the removed flesh finely.

In a small bowl, combine the syrup, cinnamon, apple flesh (if you've cut the top off) blackberries, and walnuts. Fill the apple with the mixture.

Bake in the oven for 25-30 minutes until the top is shiny golden and the apple is softened.

If the top starts getting brown too soon, cover it with a piece of foil or parchment paper.

Remove from the oven and let cool, top with a couple of blackberries and drizzle with your chosen syrup or serve with a scoop of vanilla or caramel ice cream.

Light Ricotta Strawberry Trifle

Ingredients

1/3 cup strawberries, sliced
1/3 cup fat free Ricotta cheese,
1 tablespoon whipping cream
1 trifle finger or any other biscuit cookie, crumbled
1 teaspoon sugar
1 tablespoon mint, finely chopped
1/3 teaspoon vanilla extract
1 tablespoon chopped nuts

Method

Combine the sliced strawberry and mint in a small bowl and set aside.

In a separate bowl, mix together the cheese, whipping cream, sugar and vanilla.

Place a layer of the prepared ricotta mixture in the bottom of a glass mold.

Sprinkle the cookie crumbles over it. Top with another layer of ricotta mixture followed by the strawberry and mint mixture.

Finally, top with the remaining ricotta mix and sprinkle with chopped nuts.

Serve immediately or let chill for 30 - 60 minutes and then enjoy.

Note: The trifle in the photo was topped with blueberries because I love them and I omitted the mint. I also substituted the cookie for thinly sliced brioche.

Chocolate Brownie in a Mug

Ingredients

¼ cup sugar
¼ cup flour
2 tablespoon cocoa
¼ cup water
Pinch of salt
Pinch of cinnamon
2 tablespoon canola oil or vegetable oil
1 - 2 drops vanilla extract
Handful of dark chocolate chips

Method

Add the flour, salt, sugar, cinnamon and cocoa to a bowl and mix well.

Add the water, oil, and vanilla extract to the mug and stir until smooth. Stir in the chocolate chips.

Transfer the mixture to a mug (or you could use a microwaveable bowl) and microwave on HIGH until the top is firm to the touch, but inside is a bit moist, about 1½ - 2 minutes.

Top with a small ball of vanilla ice cream or whipping cream and enjoy.

You can either turn the brownie out onto a serving dish or enjoy straight from the mug.

Grilled Coconut Peach

Ingredients

½ teaspoon canola oil
1 peach, halved, pitted
1 scoop nonfat vanilla frozen yogurt
½ tablespoon unsweetened grated coconut, toasted

Method

Preheat grill to high.

Using a brush, coat the peach halves with oil. Sprinkle a little of the coconut over each half.

Grill the peach halves until just softened and lightly marked, 5-8 minutes.

Transfer to a serving dish and top with frozen yogurt.

Sprinkle with the remaining toasted coconut and serve.

Single Serving Waffle

Ingredients

½ cup unbleached flour
1½ tablespoon sugar
¼ tablespoon baking powder
Pinch salt
½ cup skim milk
1 small egg
½ tablespoon butter, melted
1/8 teaspoon vanilla
1/8 teaspoon cinnamon

Method

Heat your waffle iron.

In a medium bowl, mix together the flour, salt, baking powder and sugar.

In a separate small bowl, beat the butter, eggs, milk and vanilla.

Pour the milk mixture over the flour mixture and mix well.

Pour the batter into the center of the waffle iron. Let bake according to waffle iron instructions.

Enjoy.

Peach Cobbler for One

Ingredients

1 cup peaches, diced
2 tablespoon rolled oats
2 tablespoon brown sugar
1 tablespoon flour
Pinch salt
2 teaspoon butter
Ice cream (optional)

Method

Preheat oven to 350F. Place the diced peaches in a ramekin. Add 1 tablespoon flour and stir to coat.

Add the brown sugar followed by rolled oats. Season with a punch of salt.

Cut the butter into tiny pieces and sprinkle over the top.

Bake the cobbler in the oven for 15-18 minutes, until the top becomes golden brown.

Place a scoop of ice cream on the top if desired and enjoy.

Peanut Butter Balls for One

Ingredients

4 teaspoons peanut butter
1 tablespoon softened butter
¼ cup (slightly heaping) powdered sugar
¼ cup semisweet chocolate chips

Method

In a small cup combine the butter and peanut butter. Mix well until smooth and creamy. Add the powdered sugar and mix well. Shape into small balls.

In a microwave safe bowl melt the chocolate chips. Gently coat the balls with chocolate and let stand for a while until the chocolate is set.

Enjoy.

Chocolate Mug Cake

Ingredients

6 tablespoons
coconut sugar (if you
can't get this then
use super fine sugar)
4 tablespoons all-
purpose flour
1 egg
2 tablespoon unsweetened cocoa powder
1½ tablespoon non-fat milk
½ tablespoon safflower or coconut oil

Method

In a bowl, combine the sugar, flour and cocoa powder.

Whisk in the egg, milk and oil.

Once the mixture becomes smooth, transfer to the mug. Place in the microwave and bake for 3 - 5 minutes, depending on the power of your microwave.

Allow to cool then enjoy.

Banana Frozen Yogurt

Ingredients

1 medium banana, sliced
½ cup strawberries, sliced
3 tablespoons plain yogurt

Method

Place the sliced strawberries and banana in a zip lock bag and let sit in the freezer for at least two hours to freeze.

Once frozen, place the fruit in a blender. Add the yogurt and pulse until you achieve your preferred consistency – I like mine fairly smooth.

Using a rubber spatula, scrape the sides and pour the mixture into a glass.

Top with a strawberry and serve.

Ricotta Mousse

Ingredients

¼ cup fat free Ricotta cheese
2 tablespoon fat free plain yogurt
1 tablespoon peanut butter
1 tablespoon agave nectar or honey
2 tablespoon chopped nuts for garnish

Method

Place the cheese, yogurt, peanut butter, agave nectar (or honey) and cereal in a blender and pulse until smooth and creamy.

Pour the mixture into a serving bowl, garnish with the nuts and enjoy.

Note: The fun of these type of recipes is that you can change things around and use fruit instead of peanut butter and garnish any way you like. Have fun!

Marshmallow Chocolate Mousse

This is a great recipe that's easy to make with a few ingredients and a microwave. Watch out, this recipe is so good you may be tempted to make it again and again.

Ingredients

3 tablespoons chocolate chips
4 tablespoons whipping Cream
2 marshmallows
4 tablespoons Cool Whip
Handful of raspberries

Method

Stir chocolate chips into the whipping cream and marshmallows and place in the microwave.

Cook in microwave until chocolate is melted. Open the microwave door every 10 seconds to avoid the marshmallows from burning or overheating.

Allow the mixture to cool and then stir in Cool Whip making sure the mixture is mixed evenly

Add raspberries to the top and enjoy!

Chocolate Banana Pud

If you're looking for a cake-style dessert recipe that's tasty and very easy to make, this is a great option.

Ingredients

3 tablespoon all-purpose flour
3 tablespoon milk
½ a mashed banana
½ tablespoon coconut oil
½ tsp. vanilla
Pinch of salt
¼ tsp. baking powder
Handful of chocolate chips

Method

Mix all ingredients on the list in a small bowl except the chocolate chips. Pour into ramekin or small oven-proof bowl and bake at 330 degrees for 15 minutes.

While warm sprinkle the chocolate chips on top of the mixture and stir in creating a crumbly dessert with melted chocolate.

Serve with a dollop of cream – delicious!

Coconut Chocolate Balls

If you're looking for
something tasty to eat
with your late night
espresso or morning
coffee these coconut
chocolate balls are
delicious.

They are no-bake and require little preparation.

They would also be nice put into small paper
cases, then into a cellophane bag tied with a
ribbon bow and given as a gift.

This is a recipe you can get the children to make.

Ingredients

3 tablespoons pitted dates
1 tablespoon coconut butter or regular butter if
you can't get coconut butter
3 tablespoons shredded coconut flakes
2 tablespoons chocolate chips

Method

Put all the ingredients in a blender or better yet a
food processor and blend until smooth.

Form the mixture into balls and place on a wax sheet.

If you want a more chocolaty taste feel free to drizzle melted chocolate over them.

Put them in the refrigerator to set for 2 hours or so.

Note: you can roll the balls in cocoa powder or shredded coconut for a different finish – use your imagination and experiment.

Pineapple Upside-down Cake

Ingredients

3 tablespoons all-purpose flour
¼ teaspoon cinnamon
¼ teaspoon baking powder
2 tablespoons milk
¼ teaspoon vanilla extract
½ teaspoon honey
1 pineapple ring

Method

Mix together the wet ingredients in one bowl and dry ingredients in another.

Beat together until well combined.

Grease a small oven proof bowl or ramekin.

Place the pineapple ring in the bottom of your dish then pour the batter over top and bake at 350 for 17-20 minutes.

A toothpick should come out clean when it is done.

Leave to cool before turning out into your serving dish. Serve with custard or crème fraiche.

Monkey Bread

Ingredients

2 Ready to Bake Frozen Dinner Rolls
1 tablespoon Sugar
½ teaspoon Cinnamon
2 teaspoon butter
1 teaspoon brown sugar

½ teaspoon Vanilla Extract
¼ cup Powdered Sugar
Splash of Milk

Method

Allow the dinner rolls to thaw just enough to be cut. Cut each roll into 6 pieces.

Mix the cinnamon and sugar and roll each piece of the bread dough in it. Place the pieces in a greased ramekin randomly. Melt the butter and brown sugar together in the microwave and pour over the dough.

Let it sit at room temperature to rise for about an hour and then bake at 350° for about 15-17 minutes, until it is cooked thoroughly.

While it cools mix the last three ingredients to create a tasty icing, drizzle over the top and enjoy.

Butterscotch Pudding

Ingredients

¼ cup brown sugar
1 tablespoon cornstarch
Pinch of salt
¼ cup heavy cream
½ cup milk
¼ teaspoon vanilla extract
½ teaspoon Scotch (or Whiskey)
2 teaspoons butter

Method

Put sugar, cornstarch, salt, cream and milk in a bowl and combine thoroughly with a whisk.

Pour into a small saucepan and set it on medium heat.

Stir constantly and as soon as it starts to bubble turn the heat down.

Continue stirring making sure to scrape the bottom, and cook for another minute or so until it is a thick pudding-like consistency.

Take off the heat, add the vanilla, scotch and butter and stir.

You can eat this either warm or cold.

Apple Cracker Crumble

Ingredients

1 Granny Smith apple
2 teaspoons butter
3 teaspoons brown sugar
½ teaspoon cinnamon
1 teaspoon cornstarch
¼ cup water
1 tablespoon orange juice
2 Tablespoons whipped cream
Graham Cracker crumbs

Method

Peel, core and chop the apple into bite sized chunks.

Put the butter, brown sugar, cinnamon, cornstarch and the apples in a small pan.

Cook for 3-5 minutes on a low heat until a syrup begins to form, add the water and orange juice and cook for an additional 5-8 minutes on medium heat. Cook until the apples are soft and the liquid has reduced to a syrup.

Take off of the heat and pour into a bowl, let it cool slightly and top with Graham Cracker crumbs and whipped cream.

Vanilla Custard Pudding with Fruit

Ingredients

½ cup sugar
1½ teaspoon cornstarch
Pinch salt
1½ cups whole milk
½ teaspoon vanilla extract
2 egg yolks, room temperature
1 tablespoon butter
Fruit (your choice)

Method

Mix the sugar, cornstarch, salt and milk together in a saucepan on the stovetop.

Cook on medium heat until it thickens up (3-6 minutes) stirring constantly.

Beat the egg yolks in a bowl.

Turn off the heat and very slowly whisk the milk mixture into the egg yolks.

Return to the saucepan and cook for an additional minute on low heat, just until it begins to bubble again.

Take off the heat and whisk the vanilla and butter in.

Let it cool slightly and place a good spoonful of the fruit on top.

Enjoy warm.

Dark Chocolate Halloween Cake

Ingredients

1½ teaspoons cocoa powder
4 tablespoons dark chocolate
2 teaspoons butter
2 teaspoons apple sauce
1 egg
1 tablespoon pumpkin puree
1 tablespoon plus 1 teaspoon brown sugar
¼ teaspoon pumpkin spice
1 teaspoon all-purpose flour
Pinch of salt

Method

Melt the chocolate together with the butter and applesauce.

Mix the rest of the ingredients together and add the chocolate mixture. Mix well until thoroughly combined.

Pour into a greased ramekin and bake at 375 for about 12 minutes, until it has puffed up.

Allow to cool before turning out of the ramekin.

Enjoy with a topping of your choice – stewed apple, cream, custard, crème fraiche etc.

Chocolate Spread Bread Pudding

Ingredients

2 slices of day old bread
1 egg
½ cup milk
2 tablespoons sugar
Chocolate spread (Nutella etc)

Method

Spread the chocolate spread on each slice of bread and sandwich them together.

Cut it into bite sized pieces.

Mix together the egg, milk and sugar.

Soak the bread in the mixture and put it into greased ramekin.

If you have any of the milk mixture left over, pour it on top of the soaked bread. Leave for a few minutes before adding a couple of dots of the chocolate spread to the top.

Bake at 325° for 20-25 minutes making sure the top doesn't burn.

Delicious with custard or cream.

Note: A delicious alternative is to use butter brioche instead of bread.

Oreo Pancake

Ingredients

5 tablespoons milk
1 teaspoon vanilla extract
1 tablespoon vegetable oil
¼ cup all-purpose flour
¾ teaspoon baking powder
Pinch of salt
1½ tablespoon cocoa powder
1 tablespoon sugar
For the Topping
2 crushed Oreos
½ container sweetened yogurt (any flavor)

Method

Combine the wet ingredients and the dry ingredients separately, then mix them together.

Mix the batter just until it comes forms a consistent and smooth batter.

Heat a pan, or skillet to medium-high heat and grease it with butter or non-stick spray.

Ladle the batter into the pan in the size of your choosing and flip once bubbles start to form on the top.

Cook for another minute and take off.

Mix the yogurt and Oreo crumbs and spread on top of the pancakes.

Note: the variations for this are endless. You can use any type of cookies to mix with the yoghurt or use plain yoghurt and add your favorite fruit. Use your imagination.

Strawberry Cheesecake in a Mug

Ingredients

2 ounces cream cheese, room temperature
½ cup sour cream
¼ teaspoon vanilla extract
2 tablespoons sugar
2 tablespoons egg whites
½ teaspoon lemon juice
½ teaspoon cornstarch
1 tablespoon strawberry jam
1 tablespoon Graham Cracker crumbs

Method

Whisk together the cream cheese, sour cream and vanilla extract until smooth.

Add the remaining ingredients and beat with a whisk for about two minutes or until it gets light and expands.

Microwave until it just starts to bubble in the center, about 1½ minutes in on high.

Remove and refrigerate for an hour or two until it has set.

Top with graham cracker crumbs.

Individual Strawberry Pie

Ingredients

½ pound fresh strawberries
2 teaspoons sugar
1 teaspoon flour
Pinch of salt
Thawed puff pastry dough (enough to cover a small dish when rolled)
1 tablespoon beaten egg or liquid egg

Method

Combine the strawberries, sugar, flour and salt.

Place the contents into a 4 inch ramekin or large mug.

Roll the puff pastry until it will fit over your cooking dish. Place the pastry on top of the strawberries and tuck the edges into the dish.

Brush with egg and bake at 400° for 25-28 minutes, the pastry should be puffy and golden brown.

Cool for five minutes and serve by itself or with a scoop of vanilla ice cream.

Blackberry Fool

Ingredients

1 tablespoon blackberry jam
⅓ cup heavy whipping cream
2 teaspoons powdered sugar
¼ teaspoon vanilla extract
1 crushed shortbread cookie
Blackberries – as many as you like

Method

Mix the cream, sugar and vanilla by hand with a whisk or an electric mixer until soft peaks form.

Add half the blackberry jam and sir through the cream mixture.

Put a spoonful of the mixture into a pretty glass then add the crushed shortbread cookie.
Carefully add the rest of the cream mixture then swirl the remaining jam through the top of the dessert.

Decorate with fresh blackberries.

Note: You can use any berries for this and use fresh berry puree instead of jam.

Simply blend a couple of berries to form the puree and use as above.

Leave in the refrigerator for a couple of hours to chill.

Apple and Oat Bake

This is a great sweet comfort food snack for cold nights by the fire. It has that feeling of oatmeal but has the dessert taste closer to an apple pie.

Ingredients

1 apple sliced
2 tablespoon brown sugar
2 tablespoon oats
1 tablespoon flour
Pinch of cinnamon
1 tablespoon butter

Method

Preheat the oven to 375°.

Combine sugar, oats, flour, cinnamon and butter in a small bowl and whisk together.

Add the sliced apple to the mixture.

You can bake this in cupcake tins and fill as many as the mixture makes or use an oven safe dish or mug.

Bake for 20-25 minutes or until the apple softens.

Rhubarb Crumble

Ingredients

1 stick rhubarb
3 teaspoons butter
3 teaspoons brown sugar
½ teaspoon cinnamon
1 teaspoon cornstarch
¼ cup water
1 tablespoon orange juice
1 tablespoon breadcrumbs
1 tablespoon brown sugar

Method

Chop the rhubarb into bite sized chunks.

Add 2 teaspoons of the butter, brown sugar, cinnamon, cornstarch and the rhubarb to a small pan.

Cook for 3-5 minutes on a very low heat until a syrup begins to form then add the water and orange juice and cook until the rhubarb is soft but still a little firm and the liquid has reduced to a syrup.

Take off of the heat and pour into a bowl.

Mix together the breadcrumbs and brown sugar and spread over the top of the rhubarb mixture.

Put small dots of butter over the top and bake for around 10 minutes until the top is golden brown

Make Your Own Cool Whip

Cool Whip is an ingredient that seems to be only available in US and is used in lots of dessert recipes. So I found a recipe for a Cool Whip substitute that I am told is as near as possible to the original.

Ingredients

¼ cup cold water
1 teaspoon unflavored gelatin
½ teaspoon cream of tartar
1¾ cups whipping cream
3 tablespoons sugar
1 teaspoon vanilla

Method

Pour the water into a small saucepan. Sprinkle the gelatin into the water, and let it sit for 2-3 minutes.

Place the pan over medium to low heat and stir until gelatin dissolves. Remove from heat and let cool completely.

Next place 1 tablespoon of the whipping cream and the cream of tartar in a small plastic bag. Seal the bag and shake it until cream of tartar has dissolved completely and there are no lumps. If there are lumps, use your fingers to work them out. You could also mix the two together in a small bowl but make sure you keep mixing until all the lumps have gone.

Pour the cream of tartar mixture into a large bowl along with the rest of the whipping cream and the sugar. Beat for around 2 minutes.

Once cream mixture begins to thicken a little, slowly pour in the cooled gelatin and water mixture while continually mixing. Add the vanilla.

Continue to mix until the cream is thick and smooth.

A Few Substitutions Suggestions

I have included this page because I had trouble translating a few American products into the European equivalents. If you know of others that I didn't include, please let me know (email address at the end of the book) and I will add them to the list.

The list is the nearest substitute I could find for the US products.

Cornstarch	=	Cornflour
Heavy Cream	=	Double Cream
All Purpose Flour	=	Plain Flour (not Self Raising)
Powdered Sugar	=	Icing Sugar
Superfine Sugar	=	Caster Sugar
Graham Cracker	=	Digestive Biscuit
Mason Jar	=	Kilner Jar

Some Simple Conversion Figures

IMPERIAL TO METRIC

1 oz = 30g
4 oz = 110g
1lb   = 450g

1 fl.oz = 30ml
5 fl.oz or ¼ pt = 150ml
20 fl.oz or 1pt = 600ml

OVEN TEMPERATURES

130C = 110C fan = 250F = Gas mark 1
150C = 130C fan = 300F = Gas mark 2
170C = 150C fan = 325F = Gas mark 3
180C = 160C fan = 350F = Gas mark 4
190C = 170C fan = 375F = Gas mark 5
200C = 180C fan = 400F = Gas mark 6
220C = 200C fan = 425F = Gas mark 7
230C = 210C fan = 450F = Gas mark 8
240C = 220C fan = 475F = Gas mark 9

AMERICAN SPOON MEASURES

1 level tablespoon flour = 15g flour
1 heaped tablespoon flour = 28g flour
1 level tablespoon sugar = 28g sugar
1 level tablespoon butter = 15g butter

AMERICAN LIQUID MEASURES

1 cup US = 240ml
1 pint US = 480ml
1 quart US = 950ml

AMERICAN SOLID MEASURES

1 cup flour = 125g flour
1 cup butter = 225g butter
1 cup brown sugar = 170g brown sugar
1 cup granulated sugar = 170g granulated sugar
1 cup icing sugar = 100g icing sugar
1 cup uncooked rice = 170g rice
1 cup chopped nuts = 100g chopped nuts
1 cup fresh breadcrumbs = 150g fresh breadcrumbs
1 cup sultanas = 140g sultanas

Thank You

Thank you for buying this book and I really hope it has given you some inspiration for simple, economical and interesting desserts to prepare for yourself.

I don't pretend to be a professional chef but I do really love to cook for myself and hope you will be inspired to start to cook fresh, homemade meals rather than settle for the TV dinners and desserts from the freezer section of your supermarket.

Remember, most of these recipes can be adapted to your own personal taste by adding your own favorite ingredients. So be adventurous and change things around a bit – this is how family favorite recipes are actually born!

If you enjoyed this book I would really appreciate it if you would leave a review on Amazon. Simply type in the title and author in the search bar of Amazon and click on the book and leave your review. Thank you so much.

If you are interested in receiving notification of the next book in the 'Budget Cooking for One' series, please leave your email address at the address below or scan the QR code to be taken directly to the sign up page.

www.eepurl.com/SZOLH

If you would like to see others in the 'Budget Cooking for One' series, simply type Penelope R Oates into the Amazon search bar and my books will come up.

If you have any simple Recipes for One that you would like to contribute to one of my upcoming books, please email me.

Penelope.Oates21@gmail.com

Thank you again.

Penny

Notes:

Notes:

Notes:

Printed in Great Britain
by Amazon